Grace
Through Every
Season

A COLLECTION OF INSPIRATIONAL
REFLECTIONS AND POETRY

---••---

Rebecca Lively Hardy

To everything there is a season,
A time for every purpose under heaven.
(Ecclesiastes 3:1)

Contents

GRACE FOR THE CHRISTMAS SEASON

A COLLECTION OF INSPIRATIONAL
REFLECTIONS AND POETRY

Rebecca Lively Hardy

Seasons of Grace

Seasons come and seasons go
Some are fast, and some seem slow
In some I rest, in some I grow
In some there i s sunshine, in some storms blow
And all of them my Savior knows

In seasons of hope, spring's in the air
With fresh, warm breezes in my hair
Tender faith grows with answered prayer
Sweet fellowship with Christ I share
New songs I sing, I know He cares

In seasons of waiting or of a forced rest
My summer-hot temper is put to the test
My parched soul forgets how much I am blessed
Oh Lord, Your kind, wise ways are always best
Preparing me for my next appointed quest

In loss or in change, when coldness arrives
What was sure feels unstable and pelting rain drives
The fearful temptation of my heart to contrive
The lie—God's love for me is no longer alive
Have mercy on me, may Your Spirit still strive
Dear gracious Lord, with me abide!

Some seasons are joyful, some carry deep grief
Some seasons span decades, some are quite brief
Some seasons are fulfilling, some seasons hold regret
Some I want to cling to, some up ahead I dread
No matter what kind of season I face
I must trust in God's lavish, unchanging grace
For it is sufficient and always enough
Meeting needs of my times, no matter how rough
He's never too busy, He's never too far
To carry my burdens, His peace to impart

He'll guide my way daily, He'll hold my weak hand
Even through those dark seasons I don't understand
Till someday He leads me into the Promised Land

November 2022

Grace
for Seasons of

Joy

Joy in the Journey

There's joy in the journey and peace on the path,
I heal the humble, give strength with My staff,
With My love you'll leap over stones that would slide,
You will not walk alone, I am right by your side.

2003

A Tribute

I have been blessed. I know it is true
For all of my life I've seen Jesus in you

For two a.m. feedings, for clothing and shoes
For ER visits and Brownie Troop dues
For college tuition and wedding day plans
When I needed provision,
You were His Hands

For enforcing a curfew, for keeping sassing at bay
For discipling poor manners, teaching me to obey
For giving me spankings and not tolerating lies
When I needed correction,
You were His Eyes

For holding my hand when I was sick
For wiping away tears after a failed bike trick,
Being there through heartaches, I've known from the start
When I needed compassion,
You had His Heart

For teaching me colors, for encouraging my growth
For looking over homework, I know that you both
Wanted me to succeed in His path yet to find
When I need direction,
You were His Mind

For carrying me across a busy street
"You'd better put socks on those cold little feet!"
Countless prayers offered to keep me from harm
When I needed protection,
You were His Arms

For cheering in the stands, for praising an "A"
For applauding a song I had learned to play
Speaking your love was often your choice
When I needed encouragement,
You were His Voice

Your work is not over, now you're my dear friends
On your faithful influence I still depend
It's my heartfelt prayer my own children will see
The Jesus you know
Living inside of me

A tribute to my parents, Darrell and Delores Lively,
on their 40th anniversary

July 2000

Daddy

When you offer help with math
Or gladly give a needed bath
Or hold small hands or kiss a cheek
And kind encouragement you speak

When you laugh with them and sing
Or when you make a toddler swing
When you endure a silly joke
Or order them a cherry Coke

When on the beach you fly a kite
Or mediate after a fight
Or share a book or play a game
Forsaking status, wealth, or fame

When you pray with them at night
And lead them to the deed that's right
When you worship God with them
And teach them to depend on Him

That's when I thank the Lord above
He gave our children to you to love
That's when I remember, too,
Why I'm so in love with you!

Happy Father's Day, Mike!

June 2005

Dear Nannie

Your love is deep, your love is true
Your love is there to see me through
Your love is sure, your love is warm
Your love is shelter in the storm

Your love is comfort, your love is wide
Your love invites me to abide
Your love encourages, your love is strong
Your love is there when things go wrong

Your love is faithful, your love is praise
Your love is constant through all of my days
Your love nourishes though I am grown
Your love claims me as your own

Your love may not always understand
Yet it is open in your hand

So on this special day that's new
This blessing I will pray for you
That in greater ways you'll know this love
From Father God enthroned above

His love is deep, His love is true
His love will always see you through
His love is sure, His love is warm
His love is shelter in the storm

His love is comfort, His love is wide
His love invites you to abide
His love encourages, His love is strong
His love is there when things go wrong

His love is faithful, His love is praise
His love is constant through all of your days
His love nourishes though you are grown
His love claims you as His own

Though His love you may not understand
He'll always hold you in His hand
Forever you'll be in His hand

Happy birthday, Nannie!
Dedicated to my grandmother, Emma Perry

November 2005

Grace

The seed of your life unexpectedly took root in me.
Other moms could have been a better choice. I'm not
The most beautiful, intelligent, or talented. Certainly, I don't
Possess the most balanced emotions, the greatest patience,
Or the most developed selfless character. I don't have a
Luxurious lifestyle to offer you. Nevertheless, you are
Here. I was chosen to bear the blessing of you.
You are the perfect illustration of God's gift
Of love. I can never earn it or deserve it.
His salvation is truly unmerited.
What a joy it will
Be to see you
Blossom and
Take shape, for
His handiwork
Of you represents
His ultimate gift of
GRACE.

August 2001

Great Day

She came before the judge alone. Over a decade ago, she had been charged with a drug offense and personally struggled with addiction for the next several years. Why did she seek this court appearance? She was requesting her criminal records to be sealed. A clean slate. I just happened to be in the courtroom that day on other business. From where I sat, I could see her earnestness. She pleaded that she had been clean for six years. She described her steps towards recovery— regular contact with a psychiatrist and support group, and a stable relationship. She had volunteered with an organization that trained service animals. However, with her lingering record, she had extreme difficulty finding a job. At one point, she confessed her nervousness and broke down—she hadn't expected to plead her case in front of the judge AND a courtroom full of strangers. The judge graciously assured her to take her time. She spoke of her desire to have a job and be a contributing member of the community. Unfortunately, this woman was shackled to a history of bad choices admittedly of her own making.

Then the judge spoke. He described the brokenness of the cycle of drug addiction and the societal consequences. He stated that recovery was possible with commitment and hard work. First the judge removed her debt towards former court costs she stated were unknown to her. What followed brought tears to my eyes.

"This is a great day for you," said the judge. "I see no reason why the county needs to keep your records open. They are hereby sealed. Keep doing a great job with your recovery."

So, was it a coincidence that I was presently in a ladies' Bible study on the Epistle of Jude? Not a chance! The popular benediction of the book reads, "Now to Him who is able to keep you from stumbling and to present you faultless before the presence of His glory with exceeding joy, To our God and Savior, Who alone is wise, Be glory and majesty, Dominion and power, Both now and forever. Amen" (Jude 24–25). Because of my faith in Jesus as my Savior, I am "looking for the mercy of our Lord Jesus Christ" (Jude 21). When I stand before God, rather than receive condemnation for my sins, I can be assured that I will have pardon due to Jesus' sacrifice on the cross. Jesus paid my debt and gives me a clean slate. "If we confess our sins, he is faithful and just to forgive us our sins and to cleanse us from all unrighteousness" (1 John 1:9). In the courtroom, I could sense the goodwill of the judge towards the woman before him. In a far greater way, Jesus frees us and presents us before God's presence "with exceeding joy"! He takes great delight in saving us. The Lord used this courtroom experience to sink these truths deep into my heart as never before. Every day can be a great day when we cherish the salvation Christ offers us. When He comes or when He calls, I am looking forward to the ultimate Great Day when I receive His grace and mercy eternally.

2020

Tribute to Educators

Did I ever say thank you for the way you cared for my young, eager mind, giving me a safe, warm environment in which to learn and grow?
Thank you,

Miss Timmer, for teaching me how to rhyme and read.

Mrs. Lucky, for teaching me how to write in cursive.

Mrs. Graff, for opening the world of drama to me and awakening this lifelong passion.

Mrs. Petkiewytsch, for teaching me long division and offering lotion for my chapped hands.

Miss Holb (now Mrs. Cannon), for being a remarkable first-year teacher who made learning so much fun and for taking the time to prepare a piano duet with me.

Mr. Lucky, for teaching me how to play the clarinet.

Mr. Spade, for handling my "gerbil mishap" with honesty yet grace and later, for very practical instruction in my in-car training class.

Mr. Thatcher, for teaching me about colors and shapes and for being patient with my lopsided, dried-out clay pots.

Miss Emerson: I'll never forget "Chicken Fat" or "Alley Cat" and I'll never forget you—you dealt with my limited physical ability with understanding.

Mr. Rowland, for the joy of music and for allowing me the pleasure of singing with my little brother in ungraded choir.

Ms. Arulf, for instructing me in how to think about literature with Junior Great Books.

Did I ever say thank you for grading my papers or taking the time to answer my questions?
Thank you,

Mr. Mooney. I didn't appreciate it at the time, but that proofreading process in 8th grade paved the way for me to be a better writer in high

school. You taught me to always look for the improvement.

Mr. Knarr, for the opportunity to learn about my family tree and the freedom to give a Latin American music piano recital.

Mr. Teets, for making science experiments in cooperative groups enjoyable.

Mr. Smittle. The owl painting I did in your class still hangs in my parents' home.

Mr. Crist, for teaching me that excellence in music takes time and hard work. That one smile you beamed us at the end of the spring concert in 8th grade was worth it all!

Did I ever say thank you for how you taught me life lessons as well as tangible skills?

I have much gratitude for my high school math teachers, Mr. Jones, Mrs. Friedman, and Mr. Engle. You never pressured me to be the top math student even though my dad was a colleague. You accepted me in spite of my limitations.

Thanks to Mr. Jackson, Mr. Ferris, Mr. Gordon, Mrs. Barton, and Mrs. Williams—you empowered me with the gift of language in all of its forms: spoken, written, and comprehension.

Mr. Maroon, Mr. Reynolds, Mrs. Meyer, and Mr. Kirkendall, thank you for brightening my life with music appreciation. You taught me how to read music and to savor its gifts. How many times have I heard a piece on the radio or hummed a tune that we performed?

Mr. Marshall, you taught me about the thrill and fun of drama. I continue to use the skills you passed on to me, and of course you taught me that "wasted time is lost time."

Thank you, Mr. Eaton, for supporting me at a difficult time. Your faith in me carried me.

Mr. Dugan, the freedom you gave me to research "any human behavior" led me to one of the greatest decisions of my life. That research paper on speech and language development decided my future profession in speech-language pathology. Thank you for the time extension, and for allowing me excused class time to go observe and interview two speech pathologists. This experience truly impacted me. Thank you so much.

To my college professors I owe thanks for opening a world of countless learning opportunities. Dr. Creaghead, Drs. Donnelly, Drs. Kretschmer, Dr. Agnello, Dr. Lee, Dr. Secord, Dr. Neils, Dr. Weiler, and Phyllis Breen, I am so appreciative of the way you prepared me for my professional work. Thanks for letting me ask questions or "talk through" my learning process. Phyllis, you taught me that flexibility with preschoolers is a must!

Thanks to Barbara Donovan, my mentor speech-language pathologist, who taught me practical skills that I continue to use daily in my work with students. You were so encouraging, and you personalized my training. What a gift you have been to me!

Though I may not have mentioned all of you specifically, please know, dear teachers, that you have touched my life in remarkable ways.

Now as I look "over the hill," I have a clearer vantage point—
I watched my parents live their lives as dedicated teachers.
As an educator myself, I have endeavored to positively impact the students I serve.
And I have appreciated the influence that gifted teachers have had on my own children.
All three of these perspectives only make me value you more.

To those who have passed from this life to live in the presence of the Almighty, I have hope that among your eternal rewards there will be the knowledge that you have blessed my life as well as the lives of countless others.

To my former educators and other educators who continue on this journey, please be encouraged that you make a difference even when you may not realize it. My teachers made a difference to me.

Please accept my sincere thanks.

September 2007

Heritage Hill Elementary, 1972–1979
Princeton Junior High School, 1979–1981
Princeton High School, graduated 1985
University of Cincinnati, BS 1989
University of Cincinnati, MA 1990

Grace
for Seasons of
Loss

He entered the room prepared for him
He saw the tinseled tree
He saw the angels, he saw the gifts
Selected so personally

His heart was light and yet so full
A smile brightened his face
For he was home and he was loved
All in a warm embrace

A time to live, to celebrate
To dance and sing for joy!
For he was home and he was loved
A wonderful day for a boy

Many years later, his call came
His Heavenly Father spoke his name

He entered the room prepared for him
Unspeakable beauty
He saw the angels, he saw the gifts
Selected so personally

His heart was light and yet so full
A smile brightened his face
For he was Home and he was loved
All in a warm embrace

All time to live, to celebrate
To dance and sing for joy!
For he is Home and he is loved
Forever God's precious boy

In loving memory of James Wallace Hardy
December 2013

Better

You gave me a voice to a beautifully sing
So sweet this way my love to bring!
With husband making harmony
Worship and thanks the melody
But if my voice can't sing the same
Still, I will choose to praise Your Name

You gave me skills to write a play
To creatively act upon a stage
How fun this way to honor You
To use this craft and faith renew!
But if my form can't act the same
Still, I will choose to praise Your Name

You gave me ears to listen and care
To offer wisdom when life isn't fair
How meaningful to mentor and share
To ease the burdens that others bear!
But if my lips can't speak the same
Still, I will choose to praise Your Name

All of these talents to You I bring
As my humble offering
Yet, when You call me to a place
Where I can only see Your Face
Still, I will choose the better part
And bring the offering of my heart
You will hold my love for Thee
I'm blessed You chose to first love me

Dear friend, you are a spiritual hero who has
modeled the grace of being better, not bitter, when
faced with adversity. What great rewards await you!

Luke 10:42

Dedicated to Debby Dommer
June 27, 2016

Quiet Strength

Your quiet strength, it speaks to me
It sings of trust, it shouts out grace
It whispers hope to see God's face
It tells your faith through all your days

Your quiet strength, a priceless gift
You loved your man through thick and thin
You gave your girls your best and then
They made you proud time and again

Your quiet strength, it will live on
In those you've touched down through your years
Inspiring hearts and calming fears
Smiling love through pain and tears

Your quiet strength, it speaks to me
It's more of what I ought to be

In memory of Grandma Marvelene Meyer

February 2007

Hand in Hand

With one Hand He guides you in His light
With one Hand He holds me in the night
With one Hand He shows you wonders fair
With one Hand He carries my every care

With one Hand He wiped all your tears away
With one Hand He gives me hope for each day
With one Hand He lifted you to His Home
With one Hand He comforts, "You're not alone."

The same Hands that fashioned our lives He gave
Also hold keys to death and the grave
His powerful Hand will set me free
From mortal flesh's captivity
The nail-scarred Hands then I shall see
One holding you and the other me

Then we shall complete the circle of grace
Our free hands clasping in sweet embrace
Then instantly we'll understand
The mystery of those precious Hands

March 20, 2004

The Father's Love

For a few years, my brother Michael portrayed Christ in a church's Easter production. Witnessing this play every year as a close family member of "Jesus" has brought a meaningful dimension to my Easter celebration. The first year Michael had this role was especially meaningful because I was sitting next to our dad.

As the crucifixion scene began, the "thieves" were first led down the aisle with the "Roman guards." Before he was seen, we could hear Michael cry out in pain as he was being "whipped" by the guards. I felt my dad almost lift out of his seat. It was his God-given instinct to respond to his son's painful cry. I believe Dad almost rose to go to his son's aid—to protect him.

Now, Dad is a seasoned believer and a wonderful father, but he is just a man. If he, being "evil" compared to God (Luke 11:13), wanted to provide protection and aid to his son, how much more did God the Father want to respond when His Son was suffering? How much restraint did God the Father have to put upon Himself to stay seated when His Son, Jesus, was being beaten and torn? How quickly could He have come to His Son's aid? Only His Almighty Love for mankind could have allowed such horrid treatment of His Son so through His sacrifice we could have fellowship with God. The Father not only trusted Jesus with suffering in order to fulfill redemption's plan, but He allowed Himself to experience the agony of witnessing Christ's unimaginable pain.

And now, as joint heirs with Christ, we can be assured He hears our cries and His heart is moved with compassion for us. We can trust Him to come to our aid as He sees fit. He might also trust us with suffering to allow for His greater glory. Regardless of the circumstances, we can be confident that His love is there because He paid such a high price to have a relationship with us.

Grace
for Seasons of
Growth

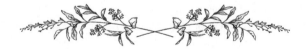

From Tiny Seeds

I prayed, "God, I want to do great things for You; I want to show You how I love You."

God replied,
"Love your children and be a good wife
Renew your mind, forsake any strife
Wash the laundry, mop the floor
Welcome the neighbor kids who come to the door
Send a card to a friend who hurts
Pray for the lost, read My Word
Prepare a meal for someone in need
Remember, great trees spring from tiny seeds."

I said, "But, God, I really want to make a difference for You! I want to impact the Kingdom."

God answered,
"Teach your children and be a great wife
Fill your mind with My truth and Life
Fold the laundry, vacuum the floor
Cherish the neighbor kids who come to the door
Intercede for a friend who hurts
Love the lost, soak in My Word
Deliver a meal to someone in need
Remember, great trees spring from tiny seeds."

I cried, "But, God, I want to do something for You that's
my own unique contribution! I want to serve You in ways
no one else can."

God patiently answered,
"Mother your children, be a faithful wife
Surrender your mind to My will for your life
Put away laundry as you dance on the floor
Invite the neighbor kids to come in your door
Help bear the burden of a friend who hurts
Speak to the lost, live out My Word
Share a meal with someone in need
Remember, great trees spring from tiny seeds."

I whispered, "Lord, may I just be with You? I really want
to know You."

God smiled,
"That's been My greatest desire for you all along."

August 2001

Spend a Little Time on Me

Am I worth the hassle
Am I worth the trouble
Am I worth the effort, Lord
Won't You spend a little time on me
Spend a little time
Spend a little time
Won't You spend a little time on me

When I look in the mirror and see myself
I'm often convicted and I cry for help
Am I a piece of work You'd rather leave on the shelf?
Am I worth the hassle
Am I worth the trouble
Am I worth the effort, Lord
Won't You spend a little time on me
Spend a little time
Spend a little time
Won't You spend a little time on me

You are the Master of creativity
I'm awed by the beauty around that I see
Some art takes more time and that must be me
Create in me a clean heart and a faith that stands
A humble spirit that heeds Your commands
Don't abandon the work of Your own hands!

You say I am worth the hassle
You say I am worth the trouble
You say I am worth the effort, Lord
And You'll spend a lot of time on me
Spend a lot of time
Spend a lot of time
Yes, You'll spend a lot of time on me

At the end of my life when Your work's complete
And in Heaven I am sitting at Your feet
I long to hear You say to me

You were worth the hassle
You were worth the trouble
You were worth the effort, Child
So you could spend eternity with Me
Spend eternity
Spend eternity
Yes, you'll spend eternity with Me

July 2003

Faithful

Faithful to follow
Faithful to heed
Faithful in service
Faithful to lead

Faithful to husband
In support of his call
In joy or in trial
To love through it all

Faithful to children
Faithful to care
Faithful to teach them
Faithful in prayer

Faithful to study
Faithful to learn
God's Word and His precepts
So others can yearn
To know the Redeemer
You tell them about
His Truth and His Gospel
Then live it out loud

When life here has passed
And the race is complete
In Heaven's blessed rapture
You'll bow at God's feet

"Welcome home, precious one,"
You'll hear our Lord say.
"I've waited to greet you
On this endless day
I've shared every heartache
Seen battles you've won
Faithful love you have given
Faithful child, well done!"

Thank you for your example, friend.

June 2008

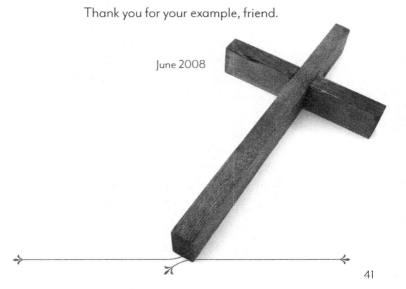

Bright Red Geraniums

In a small church many years ago
Bright red geraniums were placed in a row
Along the altar on a morning in May
That's what I remember on Mother's Day

I'd walk up to the front and with little girl hands
Give you a geranium, did you understand
How proud I was to call you mine
Out of all those mothers in that line?

Then one year for one reason or other
I was asked to present this gift to another
Inside my little girl heart I cried
Many years later my Savior replied

There's plenty of bright red geraniums for Mother
It's a tribute to her when you give to another
A priceless love she has sown in you
Give it away when I tell you to
For My true love through her won't die
It's meant to grow and multiply
Give her thanks, share your love, and be My girl
Her geranium garden will grace the world

I saw my neighbor friend in need
So I felt called to intercede
With spiritual sight not used before
A bright red geranium appeared at her door

A church friend of mine so burdened with care
Needed a meal, a hug, a prayer
With spiritual eyes I happened to view
A bright red geranium appear in her pew

At home with my own dear family
I clean, and cook, and do laundry
At night when I kiss each sleepy head
A bright red geranium sits next to each bed

Some sweet day in Heaven I'll see
My wonderful Savior who died for me
His matchless glory I'll behold
As we walk along streets of gold

Should we pass a mansion fair and bright
With brilliant geraniums all in sight
I won't have to ask, I'll know instantly
It belongs to my mom and you'll see me
Then we'll embrace tenderly
So thankful I'll be for eternity

Happy Mother's Day, Mom!

2003

Life Lessons from Dad

Perform your professional job as unto the Lord. This is service to Him!

Gifts of time and availability are more important than gifts money can buy.

Make the most of the present time. Don't let unfulfilled expectations ruin the good of the present.

Beauty is possible at any age and physical beauty is not the most important form.

Thoughtfulness keeps you from being self-centered. Even if others don't seem to appreciate acts of kindness, God sees them all!

Never expect to receive from others what you give to them. Give anyway. Discreet giving to the needs of others is the calling of a Christian.

Love means not getting your own way often.

Develop your natural gifts and abilities. Accept your limitations gracefully.

Most "what if's" never happen.

Some challenging physical work is fulfilling to do on your own. Find satisfaction in accomplishing "small" but needful household tasks.

Value a good education. It gives you opportunities and options you would not have otherwise.

Be a team player. If everyone were a first fiddle, there would be no beautiful harmony. Don't feel unimportant just because you aren't the best or at the top. Contribute and do what God calls you to do no matter how small it may seem!

Often, dependability is more important than ability. Hard work will take you just as far as if not farther than sheer intelligence. Be responsible for your own success in a class.

Honor the aged. Value their experience.

Take care of your belongings—you might want to use them again! Do not be wasteful. Use up and wear out. The latest and greatest need not replace a serviceable car, appliance, or furnishing. Be content with what you have.

True greatness lies in the ability to relate to others even if they are different than you in status, experience, or circumstances. Never think too highly of yourself to rub shoulders with people who are not just like you. Appreciate others.

I pray it will be said of me
The apple doesn't fall far from the tree
Thanks, Dad!

Happy Father's Day!

2014

Lordship

It's not about doing
It's about being

It's not about striving
It's about resting

It's not about winning
It's about surrender

It's not about knowing the answers
It's about believing the promises

It's not about perfection
It's about submission

It's not about pleading
It's about listening

It's not about me
It's all about You

For You are the Abundant Source of all
Righteousness, Goodness, Strength, and Supply
And that is more than enough to cover my overwhelming
sinfulness, selfishness, weakness, and need

You are LORD!

March 30, 2008

BE STILL AND KNOW THAT I AM GOD

PSALM 46:10

The Lesson

The pupil and the Teacher began the day. "We have a particular lesson for today," said the Teacher.

"Oh, I don't want to focus on this. I don't see the relevance," glared the pupil. The teacher reached for the written Plan.

"Here is the individualized Plan designed just for you. In order for you to clearly understand your ultimate purpose, you need this lesson. I have so much to teach you."

"Well, I have another vision," sputtered the pupil, "and it's quite urgent. I can focus on that only."

"If you insist," allowed the Teacher. "There are lessons to be learned in whatever you bring to me, but it's not what I had in mind for you today. Begin right here."

"But I want to complete this on my own!" cried the near-sighted pupil. "You'll interrupt me with your questions. I have my way of getting this accomplished. I won't see nearly as much done if you correct me."

"You don't want any illumination?" softly asked the Teacher.

"Do I have to come tomorrow?" questioned the pupil as she glanced at the clock.

"That's not my decision to make. I care so much for you, but you are free to choose. Remember, I am your Teacher and I have your best interest at heart."

In a blink, the pupil darted off without looking back. The Teacher continued His lesson plans as He waited patiently for her return.

September 2003

Broken

At a table with gracious friends
My young family sat end to end
A crystal glass slipped from small hands
Small eyes expected a harsh reprimand

Instead, his fear was met with care
A shattered glass did not compare
To the worth and safety of my little one
These friends modeled Jesus to my son

Humbled by this act of grace
I met truth I had to face
Jesus spoke down in my heart
He had a message to impart

"Imperfect pride demands perfection
You need a change of heart direction
Awkward hands may break possessions
Your sharp tongue can break a heart"

"My little ones I hold tenderly
No matter how old or young, you see
Treat My children the way you'd treat Me
Your sharp tongue can break My heart"

Lord, please break my selfish pride
And in Your grace let me abide
Give me gentleness when my patience is tried
And kind words so Your ways can mend hearts

August 2003

Fragrances

The scent of the rain
On a late spring day
The fragrance of lilacs
That bloom in May

The smell of the sea
So balmy with salt
The sweet, tasty scent
Of a large chocolate malt

The stench of rotten eggs
Or a dirty tennis shoe
In no way compares
To the smell of the flu

The new, clean scent
Of a baby held close
The spicy scent of pepper
That can tickle your nose

The sentimental fragrance
Of a bridal nosegay
Is not quite the same
As the smell of Ben-gay

Like the vast array of fragrances
We encounter every day
Our lives are full of experiences
God sends along our way

As unpleasant as some seem
Far too much to endure
In the garden of our lives
They are the needed manure

Our own goodness is as dung
Yet we long to smell so sweet
We need our gentle Savior
To tend us at His feet

The beauty of His Holiness
His lovely Breath of Life
Clears away our stench and grime
Of bitterness, fear, and strife

With Jesus as our Gardener
I'm so thankful that He chose
To prune us and to groom us
So someday we'll be a rose

With love to Mom

April 2000

Saved in the Waves

In August 2004, my family and I were at Hilton Head, South Carolina. The waves were unusually strong, and Mike had a blast out there with Carolyn and Jonathan. Then we traded spots, with Mike taking David on the beach so I went out in the waves with the two older kids. I had no idea just how strong the currents were. Jonathan got out ahead of me, and I went to grab him. Within five to ten seconds, the waves overtook us and the undercurrent washed us out to water significantly over my head. Carolyn was out there too with a small kickboard.

Fortunately, we were out there with a man and his teen son. At first, they didn't realize we were in danger. Mike also saw what was happening and ran out to get us with the other kickboard. He left David with another family on the beach. This all happened so incredibly fast. Someone got the attention of the lifeguard. Meanwhile, the man had a much larger boogie board and got Carolyn. She gave me her kickboard, and I put Jonathan between me and the kickboard.

There were several seconds of panic for me and Jonathan when we realized we were in over our heads and we could not save ourselves. I felt completely helpless. I could not save myself or my son. The only thing I could do was literally cry out to Jesus. And that's just what I did. Loudly.

It took Mike and the lifeguard to tow us in. When we got to shore, Jonathan said, "I'm so glad I got saved!" As far as Carolyn is concerned, the only way I can understand her peace and calm in that situation is that it was a complete grace gift from God. Discussing it later, she said, "I wasn't worried. I could float. And that man was coming to get me." It appears the Lord has shielded her from subsequent insecurity and terror that the enemy could have taken advantage of in her spirit.

This incident has caused me to ask God what He is teaching me. I don't think I am coincidentally doing a Beth Moore Bible study, *When Godly People Do Ungodly Things*, which is about the ability of whole-hearted, sincere followers of Jesus to be seduced by the enemy. There are several observations I would like to share:

1) The ocean was inviting. It was not cold. Others were having fun. That's the way a seduction can present itself (by seduction, please don't think only in terms of sexual sin. A seduction can even be something good, just as the ocean—remember, God called it good when He created it!).

2) I was in over my head before I knew it. I was not aware of the danger immediately. A seduction (a sinful pattern or anything that sways our complete devotion away from Christ) can overcome us very quickly.

3) By the time I knew I was in trouble, I had to admit my complete neediness and cry out to Jesus and the others around me.

4) God used more than one person to rescue me and my children. This was a perfect word picture of how the Body of Christ, His church, should operate when one of its members is struggling. I needed the support of others.

5) Not one person badgered or told me how stupid I was when I made it back to the beach—not the lifeguard, not the others on the beach, not the kids, not even Mike! Mike's retrospective comment was "I knew you had no business out there in those waves with both kids. I just didn't want to take away your fun with them." Would I have heeded a warning from Mike concerning the waves or been offended? Depending on how carnally minded I was at the moment, I would likely have been offended. More cautious, yes. In no way am I blaming Mike for what happened. But how often in the Body are we so afraid of offending a brother or sister that we see in a potential seduction? How often do we hold each other accountable in a prayerful, humble manner? While there are times in the Body

when we all need a bit of admonishment and perhaps a kick in the pants, a person who stumbles does not need condemnation. "For God did not send his Son into the world to condemn the world, but to save the world through him." That's John 3:17 (NIV). I was worth saving, in more ways than one.

6) God has proven faithful in my life one more time. He will not let me go. Praise His Name! He had another opportunity to take me out of here and He didn't. Furthermore, He must have plans for Jonathan and Carolyn. Later, I asked Jonathan If he knew I did what I could to take care of him out there in the water. He let me know that I had asked Jesus to help us and He did it, not me. I am humbled that my kids see my many weaknesses, but at least they know the Rock that stands true and constant.

7) In a strange way, this has served to strengthen our marriage. Recent seduction attempts by the enemy in my personal life have involved my negative perceptions of my husband. I asked Mike if he would have come out to get me if it had just been me in the water, and not the kids. He said, "Of course!!" My hero. That's how Christ saved me. He saw me for the needy person I was independent of my family background, country citizenship, intelligence, appearance, race, mental or emotional weakness, or abilities. He saw me floating around in the water about to perish and came to me. I asked Him to save me and He said, "Of course!!" My Hero. And my Hero keeps saving me—from danger, from sin, from torment, and most of all, from myself.

How thankful I am! God is so merciful to me. I cannot keep silent or the rocks will cry out. God is Good. He is faithful. He is my Savior.

2004

Lessons by the Sea

On the beach, there are many people from all walks of life—just like in the Christian walk. People walk in different directions, some with the light behind or above them to light their path. Others head directly into the sun. That's the way we walk with truth and righteousness. We can be going against God's ways unknowingly, and He, in His mercy, allows us to wear spiritual sunglasses temporarily. Lovingly, He removes them when it's time for us to see His truth. At first, the light is blinding and uncomfortable, as is the truth of our unrighteousness or the growing pains we feel as we reconcile our ways to God. We can quit fighting the light and turn to allow God's truth to illuminate our path. The view is incredibly more brilliant and the colors are much more vibrant without sunglasses. So are our lives when we see the truth clearly without the shading of unrighteousness over our eyes. We can truly appreciate the beauty of God's ways and plan. If we don't reconcile our ways to God, we are miserable—we painfully squint through unfocused eyes. We no longer enjoy the walk, and some may even give up and go inside. We may try to get temporary relief by looking down to the sand to be distracted by the "treasures" of life. But soon, we lose our interest.

On the shore, there are little treasures along the way that we can pick up. But if we only focus on finding the blessings, we miss the glorious big picture—the sky, the sea, and the waves. The blessings along the way are part of the enjoyment, but not the ultimate experience of the walk.

On the beach, we can enjoy the walk with others—our family, our friends, or even others we meet. We all have a commonality. We are enjoying the blessings of the walk, the Christian life. But there are times

we walk alone. In the solitude we can truly hear the voice of God. We can have fellowship one-on-one with the Creator. Sometimes we walk fast and seem to cover a lot of ground. Sometimes we walk slowly when we are blessed with a perspective we have never noticed. Then there are times we just have to stand still and be in awe of His majesty.

When we walk along the shore, we can be self-protecting by avoiding the water, or we can allow the waves to wash our feet over and over. Jesus cleanses our most vile parts, just as He washed His disciples' feet. We can lay bare our sin for Him to wash away.

Even when we are walking in the truth, God for a time may allow the clouds and rain to appear. We may experience unexplained hardships. Just because the light is not visible, doesn't mean the "Son" is gone. If we persevere, the light will return. What a blessing! During those times, we are reminded of our eternal home where no storm clouds come. Only purest light will shine.

When we stand by the vast ocean, we realize how small we are compared to God and the unfathomable breadth and depth of eternity. Just as He has placed beautiful shells among the endless shore, He has placed us in His eternal plan to bring glory to Himself.

2003

Position

One evening, Jonathan was once again saying his bedtime prayer. He was asking Jesus how he could keep from sinning. He was "explaining" to Jesus how it's really hard not to sin and asking Him how, even though He was a Man, He didn't sin. He concluded by saying, "You're up there and we are down here, and we do the sin and You do the truth." That really struck a chord with me. Sometimes the simplest insight into the Lord can bring on a fresh meaning. Having gone through a dry spiritual time (much the result of my own spiritual neglect), I was blessed to hear this simple yet profound insight. This brought to mind John 8:32: "If you hold to my teaching, you are really my disciples. Then you will know the truth, and the truth will set you free" (NIV). In support of Jonathan's prayer, I also found John 8:23: "You are from below; I am from above. You are of this world; I am not of this world" (NIV). And how many times did Jesus precede His teaching with "I tell you the truth . . ."? Maybe victorious living depends on how much truth we assimilate into our souls rather than our striving to conquer sin in our own strength. Maybe what is worse is trying to apply our own tainted brand of "right-eousness" or "truth" to a situation and falling into the relativism cycle of comparing our "lesser" failure to the "greater" failure of another.

Dear Lord, please allow me to crave Your presence. The more I know You, the more I know Your truth. The more I know Your truth, the less sin will have any place in my life. Let Your truth sink deep in my heart, Your ever-constant, never changing, yet totally fitting Word. I need You more than anything. I need You more than I did yesterday. Allow me to fully accept that I can do nothing to earn my salvation. It is all about You. You do the truth.

April 2007

Soul Cleaning

Our son David went through a time as a toddler when he did not enjoy bath time. He would cry, scream, and generally not like the cleansing process. As a parent, I could have lowered my expectations and standards and said, "Okay, David, you don't have to take a bath. You can just stay comfortable and dirty. You let me know when you want a bath." However, as a parent, I loved him too much to neglect him that way. I knew he needed a bath, whether he wanted one or not. Whose reputation would be at stake if he were left in his soiled, unkempt state? David's or mine? There were also times when he asked me to clean him up (and you can guess about those times). He knew he couldn't clean himself up, so he went to someone who could take care of the mess.

It occurred to me that God takes care of me much the same way. There are times when I come to Him and beg Him to "clean me up" because I am powerless to change myself. I know I stink and I desperately need Him to take care of me. There are also times when He knows when I need a "bath" (cleansing of a bad attitude, sin, pride, etc.) whether I think so or not. He loves me too much to leave me in a condition unfitting for one of His children, so He bathes me in His corrective grace. I may not think it's pleasant at the time, but I thank Him for taking the measures for me to be "shinier" so I can reflect His character. Just as I didn't love David less for being dirty, my Heavenly Father doesn't love me less either. In fact, He values me so much that He is willing to continually cleanse me. He wants me to be just like Him.

Hebrews 12:5–11 says,

> And have you completely forgotten this word of encouragement that addresses you as a father addresses his son? It says,
>
> > "My son, do not make light of the Lord's discipline,
> >   and do not lose heart when he rebukes you,
> > because the Lord disciplines the one he loves,
> >   and he chastens everyone he accepts as a son."
>
> Endure hardship as discipline; God is treating you as his children. For what son is not disciplined by his father? If you are not disciplined—and everyone undergoes discipline—then you are not legitimate, not true sons and daughters at all. Moreover, we have all had human fathers who disciplined us and we respected them for it. How much more should we submit to the Father of our spirits and live! They disciplined us for a little while as they thought best; but God disciplines us for our good, in order that we may share in his holiness. No discipline seems pleasant at the time, but painful. Later on, however, it produces a harvest of righteousness and peace for those who have been trained by it. (NIV)

Hallelujah! There is hope for me! God never runs out of soul soap.

Grace for the Christmas Season

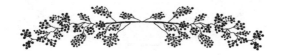

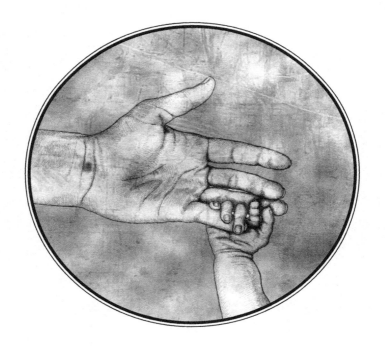

Handprints

My infant son begins to cry
Because he's mine, I know just why
He may be hungry, soiled, or wet
He may be lonely, so he frets
Such desperate pain he soon forgets
With tender care, his needs are met
While we share a sweet embrace
He reaches up to touch my face
A common love he wants to share
And so he leaves his handprints there

Long ago an infant cried
The Son of God who came to die
He was hungry, soiled, or wet
Likely lonely, piercing frets
Such desperate pain He'd soon forget
With tender care His needs were met
In young Mary's sweet embrace
He reached up to touch her face
Uncommon love He came to share
And so He left His handprints there

As God's child, I often cry
Because I'm His, He knows just why
I may be hungry, soiled, or wet
I may be lonely, so I fret
Such desperate pain I soon forget
In tender care my needs are met
One blessed day in sweet embrace
I'll reach up to touch His face
Boundless love with me He'll share
For nail-scarred handprints will be there.

October 2002

That I May Know Him

I want to know more the Baby mild
Who slept in a manger and grew to a Child
I want to know more the twelve-year-old Lad
Who reasoned with scholars, yet loved Mom and Dad

I want to know more Who made blind to see
And sat little children upon His knee
Who loved the unlovely, with "sinners" did eat
And humbly washed His disciples' feet

I want to know more this God made Man
Who carried out His Father's plan
Who denied His own will in Gethsemane
Then died on a cross for you and me

I want to know more the Risen Lord
Full of glory, to Heaven soared
I want to know more my Holy King
To whom the angels always sing

Why yearn to know my Jesus more?
So all of my life He can transform
Into His likeness so others see
That He lives inside of me

The Baby softens my heart of clay
The Twelve-Year-Old teaches me to obey
The Healer causes me to see
His love and forgiveness should flow through me

The suffering Christ shows me love's great price
Making me thankful for His sacrifice
The beautiful Savior who rose powerfully
Allows me to live in victory!

The Holy One upon the throne
Deserves my endless worship alone
No greater love could ever be shown
Than God welcoming us to His Home
Where we'll worship, praise, and adore
Because we'll know Him more and more
Through timeless ages, we'll know Him more

November 2003

The Search

I searched for joy in the decorating—putting up the
    twinkling lights, the garland, and the Christmas tree
Though this did bring delight for a time,
    the joy I'd hoped for eluded me.

I searched for significance in attending all the holiday
    parties and concerts with cheerful smiles.
Though the music was grand, the food delicious,
    and the decor dazzling,
My significant emptiness returned after just a short while.

I searched for purpose in the shopping—finding the
    perfect gift for everyone on my list
Although bringing happiness to others was a noble wish,
    I was not completely successful
My true purpose was something I terribly missed.

I searched for sweetness in traditions and Christmas
    baking—all the fun movies, activities,
And rich desserts I associate with the holiday
But eight pounds later after watching the shows and
    indulging in the tasty treats,
Sweetness in desserts and traditions was temporarily
    satisfying in every way.

I searched for connection through the company of
    dear family and friends
Though their love was so precious, sadly I realized our
    mortal connection would someday
Come to an end.

Then, I found my way to a dark stable sheltering a
    Baby in a manger
As I knelt beside Him, I discovered

Joy—for the light in His eyes overtook my darkness
Significance—for He gazed on me as if I were the
    only one there
Purpose—for the gift of His plan gave my life meaning
Sweetness—as His sweet breath warmed my cheek,
    He fulfilled every longing of my heart just by being near
Connection—for when His tiny hand grasped my finger, I
    found the eternal connection with Almighty God.

My search was over
But Christmas had just begun.

November 2004

All About You

It's not about food, it's not about trees,
It's not about garland or sparkly beads,
It's not about parties or gala events,
It's not about candy canes or chocolate mints,

It's not about music, it's not about dance,
It's not about mistletoe and a warm romance,
It's not about the packages underneath the tree,
It's not about stockings or looking pretty,

It's not about endless shopping, or about mailing cards,
It's not about decorations put out in the yard,
It's not about family and friends that I see,
It's not about dreams, and it's not about me.

While traditions and treats can be a blessed delight,
Lord, please don't allow me to ever lose sight
Of knowing the gifts flow from Your Hand
But worship is Yours alone to demand

It's about Your lowly birth on a starry night,
With hosts of Heaven's angels singing all in brilliant light,
It's about a humble stall with animals nearby,
It's about the voice of God heard as a newborn's cry.

It's about Your awesome plan to ransom lost mankind,
It's about Your healing touch that gives sight to the blind,
It's about Your wondrous love so faithful, strong, and true,
It's about forgiveness and the way You make us new.

So, Dear Lord, as Christmas nears,
Let Your truth ring loud and clear,
All about You I long to be,
Precious Jesus, be born in me.

November 2005

Be Born in Me

You were born here in a manger, oh so long ago,
The shepherds gathered 'round the stall and bent their heads down low,
Joseph's eyes were full of wonder, Mary sang her lullaby,
The angels joined in mighty chorus that echoed in the sky!

Be born in me! Let my life proclaim Your story!
Be born in me, for Your honor and Your glory!
Be born in me! Cleanse my heart and set me free,
Jesus Christ, be born in me!

You were presented in the temple, Simeon blessed You there that day,
A new star lit up the heavens fair that led the Wise men's way,
You grew in body and in wisdom, and then You became a Man,
Incarnate God gave up His life to carry out redemption's plan!

Be born in me! Let my life proclaim Your story!
Be born in me, for Your honor and Your glory!
Be born in me! Cleanse my heart and set me free,
Jesus Christ, be born in me!

Although I wasn't there to see the glory of Your birth,
And though I don't have gifts to offer that have apparent worth,
I long to know the miracle of Your redeeming love,
Restore this wayward heart I bring, Your grace is more than enough!

Be born in me! Let my life proclaim Your story!
Be born in me, for Your honor and Your glory!
Be born in me! Cleanse my heart and set me free,
Emmanuel, Prince of Peace, Son of God,
Be born in me!
Lord Jesus Christ, be born in me!

November 2006

Be Born In Me
Music and Lyrics by Rebecca Hardy

1. You were born here in a manger, oh so long a-go, The shepherds gathered 'round the stall and bent their heads down low
2. You were presented in the temple, Simeon blessed you there that day, a new star lit up the heavens fair that led the wisemens' way

Joseph's eyes were full of wonder, Mary sang her lullaby, The angels joined in mighty chorus that echoed in the sky!
You grew in body and in wisdom, and then you became a man, Incarnate God gave up his life to carry out redemption's plan!

Be born in me! Let my life proclaim your story! Be born in me, for your honor and your glory!

Be born in me! Cleanse my heart and set me free, Jesus Christ, be born in me!

Although I wasn't there to see the glory of your birth, and though I don't have gifts to offer that have apparent worth, I

long to know the miracle of your redeeming love,. restore this wayward heart I bring, your grace is more than enough!

Be born in me! Let my life proclaim your story! Be born in me, for your honor and your glory!

Be born in me! Cleanse my heart and set me free, Emmanuel, Prince of Peace, Son of God, be born in me

Lord, Jesus Christ, Be born in me!

November. 2006

Destiny

Come to the stable, all
Come now to see
The Babe in the manger here
The Almighty King!

Come see the shepherds there
Come smell the hay
Kneel with His subjects who
Worship and pray!

Come see the Carpenter
Come see the Girl
Though humble, now they hold
The Gift to this world!

Come hear the cattle low
Come see the star
Though wretched you may be
Come as you are!

Come whosoever will
Come to receive
Redemption through God's own Son
For all who believe!

He came to this lowly place
He came so we'd see
His love spans all heights and depths
To reach you and me!

He's our Destiny

December 2007

Mary's Treasure

She didn't treasure great wealth or royalty
She didn't ponder King Herod's finery
She didn't question God Almighty's awesome plan
Although I think she somehow knew she'd never fully understand

She didn't treasure great strength or rare beauty
She didn't ponder her low community
She didn't question that her load was hard to bear
But she sang her praises to the One who showed the lonely world He cared

Mary treasured the shepherds' story of how the angels had appeared
She pondered how her mighty God so loved and in His glory they had feared
She wondered how a Holy God could visit dark humanity
She was awestruck with the profound thought that her Babe would set men free

Mary treasured amazing, prophetic words of Simeon in prayer
And she pondered Anna's thankful heart also in the temple there
Later she wondered where her Son had gone when He was just a boy
She marveled at His wise response and remembered how He was her joy

Mary's treasure wasn't in the things that this world could offer here
She didn't ponder earthly fame or goods, although I'm sure she shed a tear
When her thoughts would turn to knowing God in this miraculous life plan
She treasured knowing Him from lowly birth until He became a Man

So at Christmas time, Dear Lord, I pray that I would hold You close, most dear
That I would not turn to man-made dreams at this special time of year
I pray I'll ponder Your unchanging love and the truth the Scriptures tell
I want to treasure, Lord, in knowing You, my Righteous King, Emmanuel

Luke 1:3
December 2008

The Gift

You poured out forgiveness, I gave You my sin
You love me in spite of the fear that's within

You offered me freedom, though pride had me bound
You embraced me with sweetness, my bitterness You found

You reached out in mercy, while unforgiveness I've shown
You kept me from danger, though I felt so alone

You touched me with healing, while I cried out in pain
I thought You'd forgotten, though You know me by name

When my faith's been unstable, Your holiness is sure
You're constantly giving, while my motives aren't pure

You have filled me with gladness, though I've caused You to grieve
You're still faithful Redeemer when I've failed to believe

So at Christmas, dear Lord, I'm reminded You came
This "God with us" Savior in the form of a babe
Such a precious gift to us so one day we'd see
Your glorious splendor, in Your presence we'll be

I have nothing to bring You but heartache and strife
Yet You gave me Yourself, Lord, so that I could have Life

December 2010

The Shepherds' Call

I wonder what it felt like on Bethlehem's bleak hills
To be those humble shepherds, out in the darkness, still
To keep watch over dirty sheep and to sit down in the cold
No hope of great significance from youth to growing old

I wonder what it felt like when suddenly they saw
A shining angel standing there, their senses so in awe
To hear his proclamation of a Savior's birth
To have heard the "unto you," to realize this worth

I wonder what it felt like to see the sky ablaze
With multitudes of mighty angels singing out in praise
To act on the invitation to find the newborn Babe
To run towards a stable, or a foul and crowded cave

I wonder what it felt like to see the young girl there
Exhausted with her labor, beaming tender love so fair
Towards the rough-hewn manger, joined by husband near
With careful eyes they startle when strangers now appear

I wonder what it felt like to gaze upon the face
Of helpless Infant born for all, incarnate of God's grace
To share the awesome message of angels that had come
Watching Joseph bow his head, Mary treasuring her Son

I wonder what it felt like to go and spread the word
Salvation had come at last for everyone that heard
So those humble shepherds were chosen on that hill
To bear the news to others, their feet no longer still

They teach me to do likewise, I know I can't be still
Though plain and common I may be, I have a job to fill
It is my Father's will

November 2011

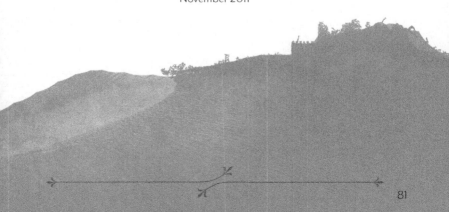

Christmas Prayer

This Christmas, Dear Lord, I humbly pray
I'll learn and respond as these did when You came

May I be submissive like Mary.
Help me believe in Your Word. Let me have a Holy fear so Your mercy will be upon me. Please remind me to always rejoice in You, my God, my Savior. Please allow me to bear Your Life so I may share it with others.

May I be obedient and humble like Joseph,
ready to respond to Your bidding at a moment's notice. Help me be willing to wait, to move, and to support in the ways You ordain.

May I be encouraging like Elizabeth.
Let me see Your miraculous Life in others and believe with them that You are faithful to complete Your work in us.

May I be awestruck like the Shepherds,
at the knowledge that a Holy God approaches me with truth and grace. Let me behold Your Glory! May I freely share Your Good News with others.

May I bless You like Simeon.
May I be led by Your Spirit and hold You close. Open my eyes to see Your salvation each day.

May I seek You like the Wise Men.
Give me the perseverance needed to travel through unfamiliar territory and even the deserts of my life. It is worth it all just to see Your face! Help me to recognize You and fall down in worship when I do. Enable me to give You the gift of a sincere heart.

Thank You, Lord, for revealing Your amazing story.
Each of these precious ones experienced a unique
perspective of Your plan. Through Your Word, perhaps I
am blessed to see a broader picture. Fulfill Your purpose
in me so I can be part of Your continuing story.

December 2012

Christmas Love

I love to wrap the presents
I love to shop with glee
I love to sit by crackling fire
With friends and family

I love to smell the cookies
I love to light the tree
I love to hear the carols ring
But I fall on bended knee

To know that You love me, dear Lord
To know that You love me!
In all my life the greatest gift
To know that You love me!

I love to read the story
Of God's wonderful plan to redeem
I love to think of how He came
Under a starlight's beam

I love to marvel and ponder
How Life, so miraculously,
Is freely given to sinners
So undeserving like me

I love to worship my Savior
I love to sing praise to my King
When doubt creeps in, remind me, Lord
To bow on bended knee

To know that You love me, dear Lord
To know that You love me!
In all my life the greatest gift
To know that You love me!

December 2013

Letter to My Savior

Dear Lord,

The first place on earth Your incarnate form experienced was a dirty, common, dark place. Yet You came anyway. You came as a perfect, holy, innocent being into the coldness, roughness, and impurity of a stable, a place polluted by animal waste. Did it pain Your Father to see You in those conditions? How His heart must have grieved! Yet He sent You anyway, fully knowing what was behind that stable door. You were to be the sacrifice for sin necessary for us to have union with You. He sent You so You could dwell in the hearts of man.

> And man's heart is such a dirty, cold, dark place.
>
> We have no righteousness or goodness of our own. We all have sin in common.
>
> I am polluted by my wasteful expenditures of time and treasure on what will never satisfy.
>
> I am dark with sin—lying, pride, self-righteousness.
>
> I am cold in my lack of care towards others who are hurting.
>
> I am rough in my calloused protection of my own will.
>
> Yet, You knock on the door of my heart anyway, already knowing all that is truly behind it.
>
> You bid me to abide with You and allow You access to my heart— in all its ugliness, pain, and brokenness. How You must grieve to know the condition of my heart!

Yet, herein is the glorious mystery—
Where my sin abounds, Your grace is greater!
You choose to work Your character in me.
You enter into my darkness, my filth, my coldness to be
Emmanuel—God with us.
Your perfect love sheds healing, cleansing, liberating light into my heart.
You claim me as Your own.
Hallelujah! You came and You are alive in us.

With love to You, dear Jesus.

December 2014

My Treasures Three

Your coming opened up my world, my handsome sons and pretty girl,
My heart has never been the same since I've been speaking out your names
Days in our home are passing by, the time has come, soon you will fly
To start your life out on your own—it's bittersweet now that you've grown

I've enjoyed our manger scene, your handprint mittens on the tree,
That jingle jangle Christmas tune, and Santa Claus who brings balloons

My times here with you since your birth have been my happiest on earth
Somehow I hope that you will know that I will always love you so
But where my sin has caused you pain, my "sorry" just can't blot the stain
Please run to God for healing balm for all the things that I've done wrong

Please take good memories for you to warm your heart your whole life through
Like setting up the manger scene, your handprint mittens on the tree,
That jingle jangle Christmas tune, and Santa Claus who brings balloons

Our times won't be just as before, who knows what God may have in store?
You may bring into my life your steadfast husband, your lovely wife,
Expanding our circle even more!

And maybe someday, as God does bless, babies will come—what happiness!
A love to know that's all brand new, resembling kids that I once knew
They may arrive with smile bright, if you allow, to spend the night
We'll paint cookies—red, white, green, blue—or make an ornament or two
We'll set up the manger scene, hang handprint mittens on the tree,
Sing jingle jangle Christmas tunes, tell of Santa who brought balloons

When God will choose some future day, I'll hear His voice and fly away
I pray that when you think of me, you'll hold a loving legacy

Oh, my precious treasures three, I must lay you at God's feet
Seek Him and obey His call, for His love is the best of all.

For my three precious treasures, Carolyn Joy, Jonathan Michael, and David Gabriel

December 2015

Emmanuel

Once again, it's Christmas time, reminding me You came,
With all the season's happy glow, the world is not the same.

I see You in the candlelight of an Advent wreath,
Your beauty in my Christmas tree with presents underneath.
I hear Your song in carols sung on the radio,
Your thoughtfulness in Christmas cards from beloved folks I know.
When I enjoy some tasty treats prepared with extra care,
I recall You are my Bread of Life when I go to You in prayer,
With snowflakes falling all around, glistening so bright,
I Know You make me white as snow when I am in Your sight.

While gazing in a manger scene at Your tiny form,
I'm so amazed the Great I AM would in this place be born.
This Son of God, Emmanuel, this Savior, Prince of Peace
Would choose to give His sinless life to come and dwell with me.

When the season comes to a close, the boxes packed away,
Remind me, Lord, You are still near, not just on Christmas Day.

I'll see You in the painted sky, Your handiwork so fair.
The gentleness of summer breeze will let me know You're there.
I'll sense Your care and comfort by a cozy fire,
I'll feel Your hope and power when I worship with the choir.
I'll know You in the kind greetings of children that I see,
And in the twinkle of Daddy's eye when he looks at me.

I'll see You in the gorgeous smile on my daughter's face,
And in my friend who points to You and always gives me grace.
I'll cherish You in the lovely tunes that my youngest plays.
I'll sense the steadfast love from You in my mother's faithful ways.
I'm thrilled to hear Your beauty as my grown son sweetly sings,
And know Your joy in laughter my extended family brings.
I'll feel Your warm and tender touch in my husband's hand,
And hold close Your forever love as I wear my wedding band.

Lord, if I but open up my eyes, what have I to fear?
The great I AM, Savior, Prince of Peace, Emmanuel is here.

December 2016

Abba

When I was a small child, a blonde curly-haired girl, I lived secure in my little world
I didn't worry about where I'd sleep, or having shoes upon my feet,
Or what I'd wear, or food to eat,
For Daddy's hands provided for me.

My limited mind did not understand all his work or how he planned,
Or all his sacrifices made, for my life, the price he paid.
My heart was safe with him to keep,
Living was simple, with love so deep.
If fear would threaten, or painful falls sting,
Daddy's strong arms would carry me.
My life secure, he was bigger than me.

In life's autumn now I live, drawn to heartfelt thanks to give
For faithful parents who modeled for me the Greatest Love the world has seen.
They pointed me to God the King, the Alpha, Omega, Maker of everything,
Who hung the stars, and filled the seas, who made the seasons, flowers, and trees.
This Holy One who wants to be my Abba Father, His face to see.
Who sent His precious Son to be my Blessed Redeemer, my Prince of Peace.

With Him, I don't worry about where I'll sleep, or having shoes upon my feet.
Or what I'll wear, or food to eat.
My Abba's Hands provide for me.

My limited mind cannot understand all His work or how He has planned,
His profound sacrifices made, for my Life, the price He paid.
My heart is safe with Him to keep.
Though living's not simple, His love is so deep.
When fear threatens, or painful times sting,
Abba's tender, strong arms carry me.
Even through the mystery,
My life is secure, He is bigger than me.

November 2017

Socks

There's a particular gift that I associate with Christmas—socks. Yes, socks.

"Really?!" I hear some say. "How mundane and unimaginative!"

Well, let me explain. You see, socks are part of the fabric of my life. It all really started before I was born. I am thankful for many aspects of my heritage, deeply steeped in Appalachia during simpler and more humble times. Christmas for my parents as children was nothing compared to what my kids knew, or even to what I experienced. There were a few gifts for fun—dolls, a sled, a toy gun made from compressed sawdust because all available metal was used for the war effort. However, Christmas was more often a time to receive needed items. Among my family folklore are stories of practical Christmas gifts— fresh fruit in hung stockings, two snow tires, sweaters, a nice pair of trousers from a sister who worked at a local retailer, certain ladies' pastel unmentionables bearing the days of the week (Saturday was always black and Sunday was always white . . . hmmm), nightgowns, a beautiful red coat, and yes, socks. Even I remember the question, "Is there anything you need for Christmas?" or thinking, "I can wait to get that at Christmas."

Giving and receiving socks reminds me of God's amazing provision in my life. You might say socks keep my feet on the ground. Socks help me to gratefully acknowledge my roots—the care, work, and sacrifices my parents and grandparents offered so that I could have a more comfortable life. Yes, socks are ordinary and common, so everyday . . . but are given with love to meet a basic need.

Long ago, a seemingly ordinary, humble, young couple came to Bethlehem, birthed a Baby in a dirty, common stable, and laid Him in a feeding trough for animals. Contrary to His circumstances, this Baby was far from ordinary. He was the Most High, Son of God in the form of a human infant. He is the most incredible, unimaginable gift to meet our most fundamental need—a Savior's Love.

Christmas is a time to receive the One we really need.
May Jesus' abundant joy, peace, and hope fill your heart.

December 2018

The Gift of Dignity

Jet-lagged and disoriented, we landed in Rome on June 2, 2019. However, we excitedly anticipated rejoining our son Jonathan the next evening in Palestrina for his performance with the Miami Glee Club, which was concluding its Italian tour.

We actually arrived in Palestrina the next evening in one piece (a word to the wise: never drive in Rome!), but I had not anticipated the weather. As we entered Palestrina, a massive downpour ensued. Palestrina, like most quaint Italian towns, was established centuries before the invention of the automobile. Its narrow cobblestone streets were not designed for cars or parking them anywhere close to the large church where the concert was to be held. We had to park some distance away— which was daunting in a rainstorm without a rain jacket or umbrella in tow. And there could be no running by a sandaled, middle-aged woman of questionable fitness and agility on a wet cobblestone street! Needless to say, we walked up the front steps of the church drenched and dripping. Several young men from the glee club were gathered in the doorway waiting for their tuxedos to arrive. Among them was Jonathan. When he saw me, he valiantly took off his rain jacket, put it around me, and hugged me, even in my unsightly condition. I was so embarrassed but grateful for his warm greeting.

Soon after arriving, a kind English-speaking Italian woman approached me and said there was a place across the street that could dry me off. She graciously walked me across the cobblestone street (she was smart enough to bring a large umbrella!) to a beauty supply store. There, I assume the shopkeeper, who spoke very quickly and exclusively in Italian, sat me down on a stool and began the process of drying my hair and blouse. Amazingly, this total stranger knew just how to fix my naturally curly, layered hair! The three Italian women present conversed as the shopkeeper deftly used her hairdryer. I have no idea what was said. Part of me imagines, "What kind of stupid American travels to Italy without an umbrella?!" or "Oh, her hair is highlighted and covering up quite a bit of gray!" All I could add in English along with hand motions was, "My son is singing in the church across the street!" However, their unimaginable kindness spoke clearly and understandably to my heart. They saw a foreign stranger in need and went out of their way to meet that need. I'm sure the shopkeeper didn't wake up that morning and think, "Today I'll dry the hair of an unprepared American tourist just to show kindness." Nevertheless, she allowed herself to be interrupted to minister to me. These gracious Italian women gave me the gift of dignity. I didn't deserve it and I certainly could not repay them. (By the way, how is there a beauty supply store still open on a Monday night in an old town in Italy?) When the shopkeeper had finished drying my hair, she topped me off with a quick spritz of hairspray. The English-speaking woman with the umbrella held my face in her hands, looked into my eyes, and said, "You are beautiful!" As we left to go back across the street to the church, all I could do was hug the shopkeeper and say, "Grazie!" I will never forget this act of merciful kindness.

What a picture this is of our Lord! Like Jonathan, He approaches me in love even in my unfit condition. Like the kind Italian women, He sees my need and cleanses me from the mess of sin. He gives me the gift of dignity, puts my face in His hands, and says, "You are beautiful!" And someday, He will usher me into His Home. Unlike anybody else, Jesus planned it all out thousands of years before I was ever born. In spite of my unworthiness and being a foreigner, Jesus provides the way for me to enter His kingdom, "accepted in the Beloved" (Ephesians 1:6). By the way, part of His plan was fulfilled in a stable still open on the first Christmas night in the small, old town of Bethlehem. Dear Lord, may I never forget or take lightly Your sacrificial love for me.

Grazie, Jesus!

August 2019

The Blessed Hope

I can't imagine the gorgeous sound
Of angels singing all around
To proclaim that You had come
That won't compare to hearing One
Who'll make His own sweet melody
When He is singing over me.

What a sight—old Simeon's glee
To embrace Messiah so tenderly
To hold the Promise now fulfilled
And future Hope of nations healed
Someday I'll join those 'round the Throne
Casting crowns to You alone.

How awestruck the Wise men must have felt
To worship the Child as they knelt
To wonder at the blazing star
That led them through their journey far
Oh, what glory that will be
When the Daystar shines on me!

You celebrated that wedding time
And changed the water into wine
You danced with friends and family
But someday will You dance with me?
Will I waltz on streets of gold
With You, the Lover of my soul?

Your first coming was wondrous for some to see
This lowly Babe that was the King
In favor and wisdom this Boy would grow
To be our Savior who loves us so
To fulfill the plan until the end
To conquer the grave and rise again

Far more exalted than Your birth
Will be Your arrival again to earth!
Your majestic glory will be revealed
Every knee shall bow, and evil will yield
Your church, Your bride will be carried away
To an endless, unspeakable, rapturous day

I'm told You're never early, nor are You ever late,
Even so, oh come Lord Jesus! I can hardly wait!

November 2021

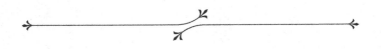

Made in the USA
Coppell, TX
16 December 2022